The YATES Senate Judiciary Committee Hearing of May 2017

Testimony on Russian Interference in 2016 Presidential Election

Edited by Richard P. Hardwood, III

©2017 FREEDOM PRESS

Printed in the USA

Library of Congress Cataloging in Publication Data

ISBN-13: 978-1546596509

ISBN- 154659650X

Hardwood, Richard P, III

FAIR USE ASSERTION

Any materials used in this book to illustrate and assist in comprehension, have been used under the Fair Use Copyright assertion of Section 107

Section 107 contains a list of the various purposes for which the reproduction of a particular work may be considered fair, such as criticism, comment, news reporting, teaching, scholarship, and research. Section 107 also sets out four factors to be considered in determining whether or not a particular use is fair:

- The purpose and character of the use, including whether such use is of commercial nature or is for nonprofit educational purposes
- The nature of the copyrighted work
- The amount and substantiality of the portion used in relation to the copyrighted work as a whole
- The effect of the use upon the potential market for, or value of, the copyrighted work

The distinction between fair use and infringement may be unclear and not easily defined. There is no specific number of words, lines, or notes that may safely be taken without permission. Acknowledging the source of the copyrighted material does not substitute for obtaining permission.

The 1961 Report of the Register of Copyrights on the General Revision of the U.S. Copyright Law cites examples of activities that courts have regarded as fair use: "quotation of excerpts in a review or criticism for purposes of illustration or comment; quotation of short passages in a scholarly or technical work, for illustration or clarification of the author's observations; use in a parody of some of the content of the work parodied; summary of an address or article, with brief quotations, in a news report; reproduction by a library of a portion of a work to replace part of a damaged copy; reproduction by a teacher or student of a small part of a work to illustrate a lesson; reproduction of a work in legislative or judicial proceedings or reports; incidental and fortuitous reproduction, in a newsreel or broadcast, of a work located in the scene of an event being reported."

Copyright protects the particular way authors have expressed themselves. It does not extend to any ideas, systems, or factual information conveyed in a work.

Editor's Note:

The Senate Judiciary Committee holds its Second Hearing on Russia's involvement in the 2016 presidential election.

Below is the full transcript from the Hearing.

Rarely do we get to realize we are watching history "in the making." I Believe this hearing will mark the beginning of one of the most turbulent and amazing times in our 240+ year history. When it is over everything will have changed. This transcript is compiled to allow the 'everyday man' the chance to read it without interference.

Read it... review it... enjoy it!

Excelsior!!

Richard P Hardwood, III

The Major Players

Sally Caroline Yates (née Quillian; born August 20, 1960) is an American lawyer. She served as a United States Attorney and later United States Deputy Attorney General, having been appointed to both positions by President Barack Obama.

Following the inauguration of Donald Trump and the departure of Attorney General Loretta Lynch, Yates served as Acting Attorney General from January 20, 2017, until being dismissed by President Trump on January 30, 2017, following her instruction to the Justice Department not to defend Trump's immigration-related executive order in court.

James Robert "Jim" Clapper Jr. (born March 14, 1941) is a retired lieutenant general in the United States Air Force and is the former director of national intelligence. He served as director of the Defense Intelligence Agency (DIA) from 1992 until 1995. He was the first director of defense intelligence within the Office of the Director of National Intelligence and simultaneously the Under Secretary of Defense for Intelligence. Clapper has held several key positions within the United States Intelligence Community. He served as the director of the National Geospatial-Intelligence Agency (NGA) from September 2001 until June 2006.

On June 5, 2010, President Barack Obama

nominated Clapper to replace Dennis C. Blair as United States Director of National Intelligence. Clapper was unanimously confirmed by the Senate for the position on August 5, 2010.

Following the June 2013 leak of documents detailing NSA practice of collecting telephony metadata on millions of Americans' telephone calls, two U.S. representatives accused Clapper of perjury for telling a congressional committee that the NSA does not collect any type of data on millions of Americans earlier that year. One senator asked for his resignation, and a group of 26 senators complained about Clapper's responses under questioning. Media observers have described Clapper as having lied under oath, having obstructed justice, and having given false testimony.

In November 2016, Clapper resigned as director of national intelligence, effective at the end of President Obama's term.

Charles Ernest "Chuck" Grassley (born September 17, 1933) is the senior United States Senator from Iowa, serving since 1981. A member of the Republican Party, he previously served in the United States House of Representatives (1975–1981) and the Iowa state legislature (1959–1974). He was chairman of the Senate Finance Committee from

January to June 2001, as well as from January 2003 to December 2006, and is now the current chairman of the Judiciary Committee of the 115th congress.

Dianne Goldman Berman Feinstein (born June 22, 1933) is the senior United States Senator from California. A member of the Democratic Party, she has served in the Senate since 1992. She also served as the 38th Mayor of San Francisco from 1978-88.

Born in San Francisco, Feinstein graduated from Stanford University in 1955 with a B.A. in history. In the 1960s she worked in city government, and in 1970 she was elected to the San Francisco Board of Supervisors. She served as the board's first female president in 1978, during which time the assassinations of Mayor George Moscone and City Supervisor Harvey Milk drew national attention to the city. Feinstein succeeded Moscone as mayor. During her tenure as San Francisco's first female mayor she led a revamp of the city's cable car system and oversaw the 1984 Democratic National Convention.

Orrin Grant Hatch (born March 22, 1934) is an American politician who has been the President pro tempore of the United States Senate, since January 2015.

A member of the Republican Party, he serves as the

senior United States Senator for Utah. In office since 1977, Hatch is the most senior Republican Senator, the second-most senior Senator overall, after Democrat Patrick Leahy of Vermont, who has served since 1975. Having served for 40 years, 121 days, Hatch is the longest-serving Republican Senator in U.S. history.

Hatch served as either the chairman or ranking minority member of the Senate Judiciary Committee from 1993 to 2005. He previously served as chairman of the Health, Education, Labor and Pensions Committee from 1981 to 1987 and currently serves as Chairman of the Senate Finance Committee as well as serving on the Board of Directors for the United States Holocaust Memorial Museum.

Patrick Joseph "Pat" Leahy (born March 31, 1940) is an American politician and the senior United States Senator from Vermont. He has been in office since 1975. A member of the Democratic Party, Leahy served as the President pro tempore of the United States Senate from December 17, 2012, to January 6, 2015. As President pro tempore, he was third in the presidential line of succession. He is the most senior senator and took office at a younger age than any other current senator. Leahy received the title of President pro tempore emeritus upon the commencement of the 114th Congress. He is the last remaining member of the Senate to have served during the presidency of Gerald Ford and prior to the 1976 election of President Jimmy Carter.

John Cornyn III (born February 2, 1952) is an American politician, lawyer and the senior United States Senator from Texas, serving since 2002. He is a member of the Republican Party and the current Senate Majority Whip for the 115th Congress. Cornyn previously served as Chairman of the National Republican Senatorial Committee from 2007 to 2011.

Born in Houston, Cornyn is a graduate from Trinity University and St. Mary's University School of Law, receiving his LL.M. from the University of Virginia School of Law. Cornyn was a Judge on Texas' 37th District Court from 1985 to 1991, until he was elected an associate justice of the Texas Supreme Court, where he served 1991 to 1997. In 1998, Cornyn was elected Attorney General of Texas, serving one term until winning a seat in the U.S. Senate in 2002. He was re-elected to a second term in 2008 and to a third term in 2014.

Amy Jean Klobuchar (born May 25, 1960) is the senior United States Senator from Minnesota. She is a member of the Minnesota Democratic-Farmer-Labor Party, an affiliate of the Democratic Party. She is the first woman to be elected as a senator for Minnesota and is one of twenty-one women serving in the current United States Senate.

She previously served as the county attorney for Hennepin County, Minnesota, the most populous county in Minnesota. She was a legal adviser to former Vice President Walter Mondale.

Sheldon T. Whitehouse (born October 20, 1955) is an American politician and the junior United States Senator from Rhode Island, serving since 2007. He is a member of the Democratic Party and previously served as a United States Attorney from 1993 to 1998 and as the Attorney General of Rhode Island from 1999 to 2003.

Benjamin Eric "Ben" Sasse (born February 22, 1972) is an American politician. Sasse, a member of the Republican Party, is the junior United States Senator from the state of Nebraska.

Sasse earned a doctorate in history from Yale University. He taught at the University of Texas, and served as an assistant secretary in the U.S. Department of Health and Human Services. In 2010, he was named president of Midland University in Fremont, Nebraska.

In 2014, he was elected to fill the U.S Senate seat being vacated by Mike Johanns, defeating Democratic Party candidate David Domina by a margin of 65% to 31%.

Alan Stuart "Al" Franken (born May 21, 1951) is an American comedian, actor, writer and politician. He is currently the junior United States Senator from Minnesota. He became well known in the 1970s and 1980s as a writer and performer on the television comedy show Saturday Night Live. After several decades as a comedic actor and writer, he became a prominent liberal political activist. Franken was first elected to the United States Senate in 2008 in a narrow victory over incumbent Republican Senator Norm Coleman, and then won re-election in 2014 over Republican challenger Mike McFadden. Franken is a member of the Minnesota Democratic–Farmer–Labor Party (DFL), an affiliate of the Democratic Party.

Born in New York City, Franken moved to Minnesota when he was four but he later went back to the East Coast and attended Harvard College. With his writing partner Tom Davis, with whom he had developed an interest in improvisational theatre in high school, he was hired as a writer for

SNL at its inception in 1975. He worked on the show as a writer and performer until 1980, and returned from 1985 to 1995. After leaving SNL, he wrote and acted in movies and television shows. He also hosted a nationally syndicated, political radio talk show, The Al Franken Show, and wrote six books, four of which are political satires critical of conservative politics.

John Neely Kennedy (born November 21, 1951) is an American politician who is the junior United States Senator from Louisiana, serving since 2017. A member of the Republican Party, he served terms as Louisiana state treasurer and took office as Louisiana's junior senator in the United States Senate on January 3, 2017, alongside the state's senior senator Bill Cassidy. He defeated Democratic candidate Foster Campbell in the Senate election runoff by more than 21 percentage points, about a month after prevailing in the state's jungle primary, along with Campbell.

Mazie Keiko Hirono (born November 3, 1947) is an American politician and the junior United States Senator from Hawaii, in office since 2013. Hirono, a member of the Democratic Party, previously served as a member of the Hawaii House of Representatives from 1985 to 1995 and as the Lieutenant Governor of Hawaii from 1994 to 2002, serving under Governor Ben Cayetano. She was the Democratic nominee for Governor of Hawaii in 2002 but was defeated by Republican Linda Lingle. She then served as a member of the United States House of Representatives for Hawaii's 2nd congressional district from 2007 to 2013.

She is the first elected female Senator from Hawaii, the first Asian-American woman elected to the Senate, the first U.S. Senator born in Japan, and the nation's first Buddhist Senator. She considers herself a non-practicing Buddhist and is often cited with Hank Johnson as the first Buddhist to serve in the United States Congress. She is the third woman to be elected to Congress from the state of Hawaii

Rafael Edward "Ted" Cruz (born December 22, 1970) is an American politician and attorney, who has served as the junior United States Senator from Texas since 2013. He was a candidate for the Republican nomination for President of the United States in the 2016 election.

Cruz graduated from Princeton University, New Jersey, in 1992, and from Harvard Law School, Massachusetts, in 1995. From 1999 to 2003, he served in various political appointee positions: the Director of the Office of Policy Planning at the

Federal Trade Commission (FTC), an Associate Deputy Attorney General at the United States Department of Justice, and a Domestic Policy Advisor to George W. Bush on the 2000 George W. Bush Presidential campaign.

Cruz served as Solicitor General of Texas, from 2003 to 2008, appointed by Texas Attorney General, Greg Abbott. He was the first Hispanic, and the longest-serving, Solicitor General in Texas history. From 2004 to 2009, Cruz was an Adjunct Professor at the University of Texas School of Law in Austin, Texas, where he taught U.S. Supreme Court litigation.

Richard "Dick" Blumenthal (born February 13, 1946) is the senior United States Senator from Connecticut, in office since 2011. Previously, he served as Attorney General of Connecticut from 1991 to 2011. He is a member of the Democratic Party.

Born in Brooklyn, New York, Blumenthal attended Riverdale Country School, a private school in the Bronx. Blumenthal is a graduate of Harvard College, where he was editorial chairman of The Harvard Crimson. He studied for a year at Trinity College, Cambridge in England before attending Yale Law School, where he was editor-in-chief of the Yale Law Journal. While at Yale, he was a classmate of future President Bill Clinton and future Secretary of State Hillary Clinton. From 1970 to 1976, Blumenthal served in the United States Marine Corps Reserve, where he attained the rank of sergeant.

Thomas Roland "Thom" Tillis (born August 30, 1960) is an American politician who is the junior United States Senator from North Carolina. He served as a member of the North Carolina House of Representatives from Mecklenburg County, and Speaker of the House, and was also the Republican Party's nominee for the 2014 U.S. Senate election in North Carolina, defeating Democratic incumbent Kay Hagan.

Former acting attorney general Sally Yates told members of the Senate Judiciary Committee that former national security adviser Michael Flynn was "compromised" after contacts with Russian officials during testimony on May 8 at the White House.

Former acting attorney general Sally Yates told members of the Senate Judiciary Committee that former national security adviser Michael Flynn was "compromised" after contacts with Russian officials during testimony on May 8 at the White House. Yates: 'You don't want your national security adviser compromised with the Russians'

Former acting attorney general Sally Yates and James R. Clapper Jr., the former director of national intelligence, are testifying at a Senate Judiciary subcommittee hearing on Russian interference in the 2016 presidential election. This is the transcript, which will update frequently.

[Sally Yates testifies about White House meeting]

SEN. LINDSEY GRAHAM, R-S.C.: ... Our two witnesses are well known and will be sworn in but Mr. Clapper, the former director of national intelligence has served his country for decades in uniform and out and dedicated his life to intelligence gathering and we appreciate that. Ms. Yates was the former deputy attorney general, is well respected by

1 people in the legal profession. Thank you both for
2 coming.
3
4 If you'll please rise. Raise your right hand, please. Do
5 you affirm that testimony you're about to give this
6 subcommittee is the truth, the whole truth, and
7 nothing but the truth so help you God?
8
9 **SALLY Q. YATES, FORMER ACTING ATTORNEY**
10 **(OFF MIKE)**
11
12 **GRAHAM:** Mr. Clapper.
13
14 **JAMES R. CLAPPER JR., FORMER DIRECTOR OF**
15
16 **NATIONAL INTELLIGENCE: (OFF MIKE)**.
17 Chairman Graham, Ranking Member Whitehouse
18 and members of the subcommittee, certainly didn't
19 expect to be before this committee or any other
20 committee of the Congress again so soon since I
21 thought I was all done with this when I left the
22 government. And this is only my first of two hearings
23 this week. But understandably, concern about the
24 egregious Russian interference in our election process
25 is so critically serious as to merit focus, hopefully
26 bipartisan focus by the Congress and the American
27 people.
28
29 Last year, the intelligence community conducted an
30 exhaustive review of Russian interference into our

1 presidential election process resulting in a special
2 intelligence community assessment or ICA as we call
3 it. I'm here today to provide whatever information I
4 can now as a private citizen on how the intelligence
5 community conducted its analysis, came up with its
6 findings, and communicated them to the Obama
7 administration, to the Trump transition team, to the
8 Congress and in unclassified form to the American
9 public.
10
11 Additionally, I'll briefly address four related topics
12 that have emerged since the ICA was produced.
13 Because of both classification and some executive
14 privilege strictures (ph) requested by the White
15 House, there are limits to what I can discuss. And of
16 course my direct official knowledge of any of this
17 stopped on 20 January when my term of office was
18 happily over.
19
20 As you know, the I.C. was a coordinated product
21 from three agencies; CIA, NSA, and the FBI not all 17
22 components of the intelligence community. Those
23 three under the aegis of my former office. Following
24 an extensive intelligence reporting about many
25 Russian efforts to collect on and influence the
26 outcome of the presidential election, President Obama
27 asked us to do this in early December and have it
28 completed before the end of his term.
29 The two dozen or so analysts for this task were hand-
30 picked,   seasoned   experts   from   each   of   the

contributing agencies. They were given complete, unfettered mutual access to all sensitive raw intelligence data, and importantly, complete independence to reach their findings. They found that the Russian government pursued a multifaceted influence campaign in the run-up to the election, including aggressive use of cyber capabilities.

The Russians used cyber operations against both political parties, including hacking into servers used by the Democratic National Committee and releasing stolen data to WikiLeaks and other media outlets. Russia also collected on certain Republican Party-affiliated targets, but did not release any Republican-related data. The Intelligence Community Assessment concluded first that President Putin directed and influenced campaign to erode the faith and confidence of the American people in our presidential election process. Second, that he did so to demean Secretary Clinton, and third, that he sought to advantage Mr. Trump. These conclusions were reached based on the richness of the information gathered and analyzed and were thoroughly vetted and then approved by the directors of the three agencies and me.

These Russian activities and the result and (ph) assessment were briefed first to President Obama on the 5th of January, then to President-elect Trump at Trump Tower on the 6th and to the Congress via a series of five briefings from the 6th through the 13th of January. The classified version was profusely annotated, with footnotes drawn from thousands of pages of supporting material. The key judgments in the unclassified version published on the 6th of January were identical to the classified version.

While it's been over four months since the issuance of this assessment, as Directors Comey and Rodgers testified before the House Intelligence Committee on the 20th of March, the conclusions and confidence levels reached at the time still stand. I think that's a statement to the quality and professional of the — of the intelligence community people who produced such a compelling intelligence report during a tumultuous, controversial time, under intense scrutiny and with a very tight deadline.

Throughout the public dialogue about the issue over the past few months, four related topics have been raised that could use some clarification. I'd like to take a few moments to provide — attempt to provide that clarification.

First, I want to address the meaning of quote, "unmasking," which is an unofficial term that's appeared frequently in the media in recent months and was often I think misused and misunderstand. So it frequently happens that in the course of conducting lawfully authorized electronic surveillance on validated foreign intelligence targets, the collecting

1   agency picks up communications involving U.S.
2   persons, either their direct interface with a validated
3   foreign intelligence target or where there is discussion
4   about those U.S. persons by validated foreign
5   intelligence targets. Under intelligence community
6   minimization procedures, the identities of these U.S.
7   persons are typically masked in reports that go out to
8   intelligence consumers and they're referred to each
9   report at a time as U.S. person one, U.S. person two, et
10 cetera.
11
12 However, there are cases when, to fully understand
13 the context of the communication that has been
14 obtained or the threat that is posed, the consumer of
15 that collected intelligence may ask the identity of the
16 U.S. person be revealed. Such requests explain why
17 the unmasking is necessary and that explanation is
18 conveyed back to the agency that collected the
19 information. It is then up to that agency whether to
20 approve the request and to provide the identity. And
21 if the U.S. person's identity is revealed, that identity is
22 provided only to the person who properly requested
23 it, not to a broader audience. This process is subject to
24 oversight and reporting, and in the interest of
25 transparency, my former office publishes a report on
26 the statistics of how many U.S. persons' identities are
27 unmasked based on collection that occurred under
28 section 702 of the FISA Amendment Act, which I'll
29 speak to in a moment. And in 2016, that number was
30 1,934. On several occasions during my six and a half

years as DNI, I requested the identity of U.S. persons to be revealed. In each such instance, I made these requests so I could fully understand the context of the communication and the potential threat being posed. At no time did I ever submit a request for personal or political purposes or to voyeuristically look at raw intelligence nor am I aware of any instance of such abuse by anyone else.

Second is the issue of leaks. Leaks have been conflated with unmaskings in some of the public discourse, but they are two very different things. An unmasking is a legitimate process that consists of a request and approval by proper authorities, as I've just briefly described. A leak is an unauthorized disclosure of classified or sensitive information that is improper under any circumstance.

I've long maintained during my 50-plus year career in intelligence that leaks endanger national security, they compromise sources, methods and tradecraft and they can put assets' lives at risk. And for the record, in my long career, I've never knowingly exposed classified information in an inappropriate manner.

Third is the issue of counterintelligence investigations conducted by the Federal Bureau of Investigation. While I can't and won't comment in this setting on any particular counterintelligence investigation, it's important to understand how such investigations fit into and relate to the intelligence community and at least the general practice I followed during my time as DNI with respect to FBI counterintelligence investigations.

When the intelligence community obtains information suggesting that a U.S. person is acting on behalf of a foreign power, the standard procedure is to share that information with the lead investigatory body, which of course is the FBI. The bureau then decides whether to look into that information and handles any ensuing investigation if there is one. Given its sensitivity, even the existence of a counterintelligence investigation's closely held, including at the highest levels.

During my tenure as DNI, it was my practice to defer to the FBI director, both Director Mueller and then subsequently Director Comey, on whether, when and to what extent they would inform me about such investigations. This stems from the unique position of the FBI, which straddles both intelligence and law enforcement. And as a consequence, I was not aware of the counterintelligence investigation Director Comey first referred to during his testimony before the House Permanent Select Committee for Intelligence on the 20th of March, and that comports with my public statements.

Finally I'd like to comment on Section 702 of the Foreign Intelligence Surveillance Act Amendment Acts, as it's called, what it governs and why it's vital. This provision authorizes the Foreign Intelligence Surveillance Court to approve electronic surveillance of non-U.S. person, let me repeat that, non-U.S. person, foreign intelligence targets outside the United States. Section 702 has been a tremendously effective tool in identifying terrorists and other threats to us, while at the same time protecting the privacy and civil liberties of U.S. persons.

And as the — as Chairman Graham indicated, Section 702 is due for reauthorization by Congress this year. It was renewed in 2012 for five years and it expires on 31 December of this year. With so many misconceptions flying around, it would be tragic for Section 702 to become a casualty of misinformation and for us to lose a tool that is so vital to the safety of this nation.

In conclusion, Russia's influence activities in the run-up to the 2016 election constituted the high water mark of their long running efforts since the 1960s to disrupt and influence our elections. They must be congratulating themselves for having exceeded their wildest expectations with a minimal expenditure of resource. And I believe they are now emboldened to continue such activities in the future both here and around the world, and to do so even more intensely.

1 If there has ever been a clarion call for vigilance and
2 action against a threat to the very foundation of our
3 democratic political system, this episode is it.
4
5 I hope the American people recognize the severity of
6 this threat and that we collectively counter it before it
7 further erodes the fabric of our democracy.
8
9 I'll now turn to my former colleague, Acting Attorney
10 General Sally Yates, for any remarks that she has to
11 make.
12
13 **YATES**: Thank you. Chairman Graham, Ranking
14 Member Whitehouse and distinguished members of
15 the subcommittee, I'm pleased to appear before you
16 this afternoon on this critically important topic of
17 Russian interference in our last presidential election
18 and the related topics that this subcommittee is
19 investigating.
20
21 For 27 years, I was honored to represent the people of
22 the United States with the Department of Justice. I
23 began as an assistant United States attorney in
24 Atlanta in the fall of 1989, and like all prosecutors, I
25 investigated and tried cases and worked hard to try to
26 ensure the safety of our communities and that those
27 who violated our laws were held accountable. Over
28 time, through five Republican and Democratic
29 administrations, I assumed greater leadership
30 positions within the department.

1

2 In the U.S. Attorney's Office in Atlanta, I served as

3 chief of the fraud and public corruption section as

4 first assistant United States attorney and then was

5 appointed United States attorney. And then, I had the

6 privilege of serving as deputy attorney general for a

7 little over two years, and finally, the current

8 administration asked me to stay on as acting attorney

9 general.

10

11 Throughout my time at the department, I was

12 incredibly fortunate to be able to work with the

13 talented career men and women at the Department of

14 Justice, who followed the facts and applied the law

15 with tremendous care and dedication and who are, in

16 fact, the backbone of the Department of Justice.

17

18 And at every step, in every position, from AUSA to

19 acting attorney general, I always try to carry out my

20 responsibility to seek justice in a way that would

21 engender the trust and the confidence of the people

22 whom I served. I want to thank this subcommittee for

23 conducting an impartial and thorough investigation

24 of this vitally important topic.

25

26 The efforts by a foreign adversary to interfere and

27 undermine our Democratic processes and — and

28 those of our allies pose a serious threat to all

29 Americans. This hearing and others this

30 subcommittee has conducted and will be conducting

1   in the future are an important bipartisan step in
2   understanding the threat and the best ways to
3   confront it going forward.

4

5   As the intelligence community assessed in its January
6   of 2017 report, Russia will continue to develop
7   capabilities to use against the United States and we
8   need to be ready to meet those threats. I sincerely
9   appreciate the opportunity to take part in today's
10   discussion.

11

12   Now, I want to note that in my answers today, I
13   intend to be as fulsome and as comprehensive as
14   possible, while respecting my legal and ethical
15   boundaries. As the subcommittee understands, many
16   of the topics of interest today concern classified
17   information that I cannot address in this public
18   setting.

19

20   My duty to protect classified information applies just
21   as much as a former official, as it did when I led the
22   department. In addition, I'm obviously no longer with
23   the Department of Justice and I am not authorized to
24   generally discuss deliberations within DOJ or more
25   broadly, within the executive branch, particularly on
26   matters that may be the subject of ongoing
27   investigations.

28

29   I take those obligations very seriously. And I
30   appreciate the subcommittee's shared interest in

protecting classified information and preserving the integrity of any investigations that the Department of Justice may now be conducting.

I look forward to answering your questions. Thank you.

GRAHAM: Senator Grassley, would you like to make a statement?

SEN. CHARLES E. GRASSLEY, R-IOWA: (inaudible)

GRAHAM: OK.

GRASSLEY: I don't want to.

GRAHAM: OK.

GRASSLEY: I've got questions.

GRAHAM: All right, you'll get to ask them. Senator Feinstein?

SEN. DIANNE FEINSTEIN, D-CALIF.: Thank you very much, Mr. Chairman and I'll be very brief. We have prepared for the committee and I'd like to ask the staff to distribute it, a background and timeline on Lieutenant General Michael Flynn and some of the key dates involved, which may be of help to the subcommittee.

1

2 And I would just like to take this opportunity to

3 thank the subcommittee, Chairman Graham and —

4 and the Ranking Member Whitehouse, I think you've

5 done a good job and your whole subcommittee has.

6 And so thank you very, very much.

7

8 I'd just like to make a few comments, if I might, and

9 put all the remarks in the record. I think it is a

10 foregone conclusion about Russia's involvement and

11 we see it replicated even in the French election,

12 perhaps not to the extent or in the way, but certainly

13 replicated.

14

15 On February 9th, 2017, the Washington Post reported

16 that either Flynn had misled the vice president or that

17 Pence had misspoken. Lieutenant General Flynn

18 resigned his post on February 13th, four days after the

19 Post broke this story. There are still many

20 unanswered questions about General Flynn,

21 including who know what — who knew what and

22 when.

23

24 For example, the press is now reporting that in

25 addition to the warning from Sally Yates, concerns

26 were raised by former President Obama directly to

27 then President-elect Trump, 95 days before Flynn

28 resigned. So the question, what role did Flynn play in

29 communications with the Russians, both after the first

30 warning by President Obama and then after the

warning by Sally Yates? And I hope to ask that today. What role did Flynn play in high-level national security decisions, again both during the 95 days and the 18 days when the White House was on notice?

So, I look forward to hearing more about this from you, acting Attorney General Yates. You have stated that you warned the White House on January 26, nearly three weeks before Flynn resigned that he had not been truthful and might be vulnerable to Russian blackmail.

And finally, there are other troubling questions regarding Russia's relationships and connections with Trump advisors and associates. And there are questions about whether anyone was the target of Russian intelligence, either to be exploited or cultivated.

So, I will put my whole remarks in the record, Mr. Chairman. And I hope to ask some questions around these few comments. Thank you very much for this opportunity.

GRAHAM: Yes, ma'am, without objections.

SEN. SHELDON WHITEHOUSE, D-R.I.: Mr. Chairman, may I also put into the record a letter dated November 18, 2016 from the ranking member on the House Committee on Oversight Government

1 Reform, Representative Elijah Cummings, giving then
2 Vice President-elect Pence notice about certain —
3 what he called apparent conflicts of interest regarding
4 General Flynn?

6 **GRAHAM:** Without objection. General Clapper, on
7 March 5, 2017, you said the following to a question.
8 Here's the question.

10 Does intelligence exist that can definitely answer the
11 following question, whether there were improper
12 contacts between the Trump campaign and Russian
13 officials? You said we did not include any evidence in
14 our report.

16 And I say our, that's the NSA, the FBI, the CIA, with
17 my office, the Director of National Intelligence, that
18 had anything — that had any reflection of collusion
19 between members of the Trump campaign and the
20 Russians. There was no evidence of that included in
21 our report.

23 Chuck Todd (ph) then asked, I understand that, but
24 does it exist? You say no, not to my knowledge. Is
25 that still accurate?

27 **CLAPPER:** It is.

29 **GRAHAM:** Ms. Yates, do you have any evidence —
30 are you aware of any evidence that would suggest

that in the 2016 campaign anybody in the Trump campaign colluded — colluded with the Russian government intelligence services in improper fashion?

YATES: And Senator, my answer to that question would require me to reveal classified information. And so, I — I can't answer that.

GRAHAM: Well, I don't get that because he just said he issued the report. And he said he doesn't know of any. So, what would you know that's not in the report?

(CROSSTALK)

CLAPPER: Are you asking me, or ...

GRAHAM: No, her.

CLAPPER: Oh.

YATES: Well, I think that Director Clapper also said that he was unaware of the FBI counter intelligence investigations.

GRAHAM: Would it be fair to say that the counter-intelligence investigation was not mature enough to come to his — to get in the report. Is that fair, Mr. — Mr. Clapper?

1

2 **CLAPPER:** I — that's an — that's a possibility.

3

4 **GRAHAM:** What I don't get is how the FBI can have
5 a counter- intelligence investigation suggesting
6 collusion, and you, as director of National Intelligence
7 not know about it, and the FBI sign on to a report that
8 basically said there was no collusion.

9

10 **CLAPPER:** I can only speculate why that's so. There
11 wasn't — the evidence, if there was any, didn't reach
12 the evidentiary bar in terms of the level of confidence
13 that we were striving for in that intelligence
14 community assessment.

15

16 **GRAHAM:** OK, that makes perfect sense to me.
17 Follow up on that, are you familiar with a dossier
18 about Mr. Trump compiled with some guy in
19 England?

20

21 **CLAPPER:** I am.

22

23 **GRAHAM:** Did you find that to be a credible report?

24

25 **CLAPPER:** Well, we didn't make a judgment on that.
26 And that's — that's one reason why we did not
27 include it in the body of our intelligence community
28 assessment.

29

1 **GRAHAM:** You didn't find it credible enough to be
2 included?

3

4 **CLAPPER:** We couldn't corroborate the sourcing,
5 particularly the second -- third-order sources.

6

7 **GRAHAM:** Ms. Yates, are you familiar with the
8 dossier?

9

10 **YATES**: (OFF-MIKE)

11

12 **CLAPPER:** Microphone.

13

14 **GRAHAM:** Microphone.

15

16 **YATES**: If I could try to clarify one answer before as
17 well, because I think, Senator Graham, you may have
18 misunderstood me. You asked me whether I was
19 aware of any evidence of collusion, and I declined to
20 answer because answering would reveal classified
21 information.

22

23 I believe that that's the same answer that Director
24 Comey gave to this committee when he was asked
25 this question as well. And he made clear, and I'd like
26 to make clear, that just because I say I can't answer it,
27 you should not draw from that an assumption that
28 that means that the answer is yes.

29

30 **GRAHAM:** OK, fair enough.

1

2 **CLAPPER:** I also think, if I may, sir, that this
3 illustrates what I was trying to get at in my statement
4 about the unique position that FBI straddles between
5 intelligence and law enforcement.

6

7 **GRAHAM:** I just want the country to know that
8 whatever they're doing on the counterintelligence
9 side, Mr. Clapper didn't know about it, didn't make it
10 in the report and we'll see what comes from it. Ms.
11 Yates, what did you tell the White House about Mr.
12 Flynn?

13

14 **YATES**: I had two in-person meetings and one phone
15 call with the White House Counsel about Mr. Flynn.
16 The first meeting occurred on January 26, called Don
17 McGahn first thing that morning and told him that I
18 had a very sensitive matter that I needed to discuss
19 with him, that I couldn't talk about it on the phone
20 and that I needed to come see him. And he agreed to
21 meet with me later that afternoon.

22

23 I took a senior member of the national security
24 division who was overseeing this matter with me to
25 meet with Mr. McGahn. We met in his office at the
26 White House which is a skiff (ph) so we could discuss
27 classified information in his office. We began our
28 meeting telling him that there had been press
29 accounts of statements from the vice president and

others that related conduct that Mr. Flynn had been involved in that we knew not to be the truth.

And as I - as I tell you what happened here, again I'm going to be very careful not to reveal classified information.

GRAHAM: Well the reason you knew it wasn't true was because you had collected some intelligence from an incidental collection system, is that fair to say?

YATES: And I can't answer that because that again would call me - for me to reveal classified information.

GRAHAM: Let me ask you this, did anybody ever make a request to unmask the conversation between the Russian ambassador and Mr. Flynn?

YATES: And again, Senator, I can't answer a question like that, it would call for classified information...

GRAHAM: ...Mr. Clapper, do you know if that was the case?

CLAPPER: I don't.

GRAHAM: Is there a way to find that out?

1   **CLAPPER:** Well, in another setting it could be
2   discussed.
3
4   **GRAHAM:** But there is a record somewhere of who
5   would make a request to unmask the conversation
6   with General Flynn and the Russian ambassador?
7
8   **CLAPPER:** Well, I'm...
9
10 **GRAHAM:** ...If one was made, there'd be a record of
11 it?
12
13 **CLAPPER:** I can't speak to this specific case but I can
14 generally
15 comment that in the case of 702 requests, yes, those
16 are all documented.
17
18 **GRAHAM:** OK and I don't mean to interrupt you but
19 this is important to me. How did the conversation
20 between the Russian ambassador and Mr. Flynn make
21 it to the "Washington Post?"
22
23 **YATES**: Which one of us are you asking?
24
25 **GRAHAM:** Ms. Yates.
26
27 **CLAPPER:** That's a great question.
28
29 **GRAHAM:** I thought so...
30

1　**CLAPPER:** ...All of us would like to know that and I
2　don't know the answer to that.
3
4　**YATES**: Yeah. Nor do I know the answer to that.
5
6　**GRAHAM:** Is it fair to say that if somebody did make
7　an unmasking request, we would know who they
8　were and we could find out from them who they
9　shared the information with? Is that fair to say, the
10　system would allow us to do what I just described?
11
12　**YATES**: Well, unmasking requests are not made to
13　the Department of Justice.
14
15　**GRAHAM:** No but to the agency who does the
16　collection.
17
18　**YATES**: That's my understanding is that yes...
19
20　**GRAHAM:** ...So there should be a record somewhere
21　in our system whether or not an unmasking request
22　was made for the conversation between Mr. Flynn
23　and the Russian ambassador. We should be ale to
24　determine if it did - if it was made, who made it. Then
25　we can ask, what did they do with the information? Is
26　that a fair statement, Mr. Clapper?
27
28　**CLAPPER:** Yes.
29

GRAHAM: OK. Now what did you finish? What did you tell the White House?

YATES: So I told them again that there were a number of press accounts of statements that had been made by the vice president and other high-ranking White House officials about General Flynn's conduct that we knew to be untrue. And we told them how we knew that this - how we had this information, how we had acquired it, and how we knew that it was untrue.

And we walked the White House Counsel who also had an associate there with him through General Flynn's underlying conduct, the contents of which I obviously cannot go through with you today because it's classified. But we took him through in a fair amount of detail of the underlying conduct, what General Flynn had done, and then we walked through the various press accounts and how it had been falsely reported.

We also told the White House Counsel that General Flynn had been interviewed by the FBI on February 24. Mr. McGahn asked me how he did and I declined to give him an answer to that. And we then walked through with Mr. McGahn essentially why we were telling them about this and the first thing we did was to explain to Mr. McGahn that the underlying conduct that General Flynn had engaged in was problematic in and of itself.

Secondly, we told him we felt like the vice president and others were entitled to know that the information that they were conveying to the American people wasn't true. And we wanted to make it really clear right out of the gate that we were not accusing Vice President Pence of knowingly providing false information to the American people.

And, in fact, Mr. McGahn responded back to me to let me know that anything that General Flynn would've said would have been based -- excuse me -- anything that Vice President Pence would have said would have been based on what General Flynn had told him.

We told him the third reason was -- is because we were concerned that the American people had been misled about the underlying conduct and what General Flynn had done, and additionally, that we weren't the only ones that knew all of this, that the Russians also knew about what General Flynn had done.

And the Russians also knew that General Flynn had misled the vice president and others, because in the media accounts, it was clear from the vice president and others that they were repeating what General Flynn had told them, and that this was a problem

1 because not only did we believe that the Russians
2 knew this, but that they likely had proof of this
3 information.
4
5 And that created a compromise situation, a situation
6 where the national security adviser essentially could
7 be blackmailed by the Russians. Finally, we told them
8 that we were giving them all of this information so
9 that they could take action, the action that they
10 deemed appropriate.
11
12 I remember that Mr. McGahn asked me whether or
13 not General Flynn should be fired, and I told him that
14 that really wasn't our call, that was up to them, but
15 that we were giving them this information so that
16 they could take action, and that was the first meeting.
17
18 **GRAHAM:** Thank you, and I'll go to Senator
19 Whitehouse -- one very quick question. Was...
20
21 **YATES**: Yeah.
22
23 **GRAHAM:** ... are you either one of you aware of
24 incidental collection by our intelligence community --
25 of any presidential candidate, staff or campaign
26 during the 2016 election cycle?
27
28 **CLAPPER:** Say that again, sir. I'm sorry (ph).
29

1   **GRAHAM:** Was there any incidental collection,
2   where our intelligence community collects
3   information, involving a presidential candidate on
4   either side of the aisle during 2015 or 2016?
5
6   **CLAPPER:** No, not to my knowledge.
7
8   **YATES**: I believe Director Comey was also asked this
9   question and declined to answer it, so I'm -- I need to
10   follow the same lines the DOJ has drawn. Again, you
11   should not draw from that that my answer is yes, but
12   rather, that the answer would require me to reveal
13   classified information.
14
15   **GRAHAM:** Thank you.
16   Senator Whitehouse.
17
18   **CLAPPER:** My -- my response is all within the
19   context of intelligence -- foreign intelligence, not the
20   domestic consideration.
21
22   **YATES**: (OFF-MIKE)
23
24   **GRAHAM:** Exactly.
25
26   **WHITEHOUSE:** Following the Comey line, the
27   director testified a few days ago in the full committee
28   that the FBI had interviewed Mr. Flynn a day before,
29   or two days before, your meeting at the White House,
30   and you've just testified that you had told the White

1 House counsel that the FBI had interviewed Flynn
2 and he'd asked -- McGahn had asked, how'd he do?
3
4 **YATES**: Right.
5
6 **WHITEHOUSE:** Did you have the 302 with you
7 when you were in the White House? Did you show it
8 to White House counsel? And had you seen it at the
9 time you went up to the White House?
10
11 **YATES**: No. The FBI had conducted the interview on
12 the 24th. We got a readout from the FBI on the 25th, a
13 detailed readout specifically from the agents that had
14 conducted the interview.
15
16 But we didn't want to wait for the 302, because we felt
17 that it was important to get this information to the
18 White House as quickly as possible, so we had folks
19 from the national security division who spent a lot of
20 time with the agents, not only finding out exactly how
21 the interview went but how this impacted their
22 investigation.
23
24 **WHITEHOUSE:** So did you take that summary with
25 you? Do you have any document with you that
26 described the FBI interview of General Flynn?
27
28 **YATES**: At the time that I was there, I had notes that
29 described that interview, as well as the individual
30 that was with me -- the senior career official from the

1   national security division -- had been part of all of
2   those discussions with the FBI.
3
4   **WHITEHOUSE:** Did you discuss criminal
5   prosecution of Mr. Flynn -- General Flynn?
6
7   **YATES**: My recollection is that did not really come up
8   much in the first meeting. It did come up in the
9   second meeting, when Mr. McGahn called me back
10 the next morning and asked the -- the morning after --
11 this is the morning of the 27th, now -- and asked me if
12 I could come back to his office.
13
14 And so I went back with the NSD official, and there
15 were essentially four topics that he wanted to discuss
16 there, and one of those topics was precisely that. He
17 asked about the applicability of certain statutes,
18 certain criminal statutes and, more specifically,
19 about...
20
21 **WHITEHOUSE:** This was (ph) the second meeting at
22 the White House Counsel's Office in his office again?
23
24 **YATES**: In his office again.
25
26 **WHITEHOUSE:** With the same two individuals?
27
28 **YATES**: Exactly.
29
30 **WHITEHOUSE:** On the following day?

1

2   **YATES**: Right.

3

4   **WHITEHOUSE:** And you went back pursuant to a

5   phone call request or a -- was...

6

7   **YATES**: Yes, the morning of the 27th after our

8   meeting had occurred on the afternoon of the 26th,

9   the morning of the 27th, Mr. McGahn called me and

10 asked if I could come back to the White House to

11 discuss this further. And we set up a time and I went

12 over there that afternoon, bringing again the same

13 career official with me from the national security

14 division, who was overseeing this investigation.

15

16 He had the same associate from the White House

17 Counsel's Office and we talked through four to five

18 more issues.

19

20 **WHITEHOUSE:** You could perhaps have waited

21 until you actually had seen the agents 302 from the

22 interview of General Flynn. Why go ahead of that?

23 Why not wait?

24

25 **YATES**: Well, because this was a matter of some

26 urgency, we...

27

28 **WHITEHOUSE:** Describe.

29

1 **YATES**: In making the determination about
2 notification here, we had to balance a variety of
3 interest. For the reasons that I just described a few
4 minutes ago, we felt like it was critical that we get this
5 information to the White House, because in part
6 because the vice president was unknowingly making
7 false statements to the public and because we
8 believed that General Flynn was compromised with
9 respect to the Russians.
10
11 We were balancing this though, against the FBI's
12 investigation, as you would always do, and take into
13 account the investigating agency's desires and
14 concerns about how a notification might impact that
15 ongoing investigation. But once General Flynn was
16 interviewed, there was no longer a concern about an
17 impact on an investigation.
18
19 **WHITEHOUSE:** Do you know where that interview
20 took place or under what circumstances?
21
22 **YATES**: I believe it took place at the White House.
23
24 **WHITEHOUSE:** The Flynn interview?
25
26 **YATES**: Yes.
27
28 **WHITEHOUSE:** OK. Do you know if Flynn was
29 represented by council at the time?
30

1 **YATES**: I don't believe he was.

2

3 **WHITEHOUSE:** OK. And the scenario that you were
4 concerned about was that you were seeing all these
5 statements coming from the White House that were
6 inconsistent with what you knew, you presumed that
7 the White House was being truthful which meant that
8 Flynn was misleading them.

9

10 **YATES**: Right.

11

12 **WHITEHOUSE:** Which meant that he was vulnerable
13 to manipulation by the Russians, who knowing what
14 had actually taken place could call up the national
15 security advisor to the president and say, you got to
16 do this for us or we're going to out you with all your
17 folks and your career is done.

18

19 **YATES**: That's right, because one of the questions that
20 Mr. McGahn asked me when I went back over the
21 second day was essentially, why does it matter to DOJ
22 if one White House official lies to another White
23 House official?

24

25 And so we explained to him, it was a whole lot more
26 than that and went back over the same concerns that
27 we had raised with them the prior day, that the
28 concern first about the underlying conduct itself, that
29 he had lied to the vice president and others, the
30 American public had been misled.

1
2 And then importantly, that every time this lie was
3 repeated and the misrepresentations were getting
4 more and more specific, as -- as they were coming
5 out. Every time that happened, it increased the
6 compromise and to state the obvious, you don't want
7 your national security advisor compromised with the
8 Russians.
9
10 **WHITEHOUSE:** Were there any takeaways from the
11 first meeting or action items that you left with?
12
13 **YATES**: Well, there was an action item in the second
14 meeting because I got -- we talked about several
15 issues but...
16 **WHITEHOUSE:** To get the order right, you said
17 earlier that there were two meetings and a phone call.
18
19 **YATES**: Right.
20
21 **WHITEHOUSE:** Was the phone call the phone call
22 that set up the second meeting or was there a third...
23
24 **YATES**: There was a third substantive phone call.
25 There was a...
26
27 **WHITEHOUSE:** Go ahead, I can...
28
29 **YATES**: Sorry about that. One of the -- one of the
30 issues that Mr. McGahn raised with me in this second

1 meeting that again was on the 27th, the day after the
2 first meeting, was his concern because we had told
3 him before that we were giving him this information
4 so that they could take action.
5
6 And he said that they were concerned that taking
7 action might interfere with the FBI investigation. And
8 we told him, both the senior career official and I, that
9 he should not be concerned with it, that General
10 Flynn had been interviewed, that their action would
11 not interfere with any investigation and in fact, I
12 remember specifically saying, you know it wouldn't
13 really be fair of us to tell you this and then expect you
14 to sit on your hands.
15
16 **WHITEHOUSE:** Was the interview of General Flynn
17 accelerated once you became aware of this
18 information and felt you needed to get his statement
19 quickly?
20
21 **YATES**: Well, we had wanted to tell the White House
22 as quickly as possible and we're working with the FBI
23 and in the course of the investigation but certainly,
24 we did...
25
26 **(CROSSTALK)**
27
28 **WHITEHOUSE:** And the first thing you know is that
29 you have information that one thing was said and the
30 White House is saying something different. And you

1 know that that information irrespective of who is
2 involved needs to get up to the White House quickly.
3 And so at that point, the decision was made to do the
4 interview so that that was locked down before you
5 went up to White House counsel?
6
7 **YATES**: Right, so that that would not have a negative
8 impact on the FBI investigation at that point.
9
10 And there was a request made by Mr. McGahn, in the
11 second meeting as to whether or not they would be
12 able to look at the underlying evidence that we had
13 that we had described for him of General Flynn's
14 conduct. And we told him that we were inclined to
15 allow them to look at that underlying evidence, that
16 we wanted to go back to DOJ and be able to make the
17 logistical arrangements for that. This second meeting
18 on the 27th occurred late in the afternoon, this is
19 Friday the 27th. So we told him that we would work
20 with the FBI over the weekend on this issue and get
21 back with him on Monday morning. And I called him
22 first thing Monday morning to let him know that we
23 would allow them to come over and to review the
24 underlying evidence.
25
26 **WHITEHOUSE:** And was that the phone call or is
27 there a separate phone call?
28
29 **YATES**: There was the phone call initially to let him
30 know I needed to come see him.

1

2 **WHITEHOUSE:** Yeah?

3 **YATES**: Two meetings and then a phone call at the

4 end to let him know...

5

6 **WHITEHOUSE:** That the material was available if he

7 wanted to see it.

8

9 **YATES**: ... that the material was available. He had to

10 call me back. He was not available then and I did not

11 hear back from him until that afternoon of Monday

12 the 30th.

13

14 **WHITEHOUSE:** And that was the end of this

15 episode, nobody came over to look at the material?

16

17 **YATES**: I don't know what happened after that

18 because that was my last day with DOJ.

19

20 **WHITEHOUSE:** Got it. OK.

21 (LAUGHTER)

22

23 **GRAHAM:** Senator Grassley.

24

25 **GRASSLEY:** Mr. Clapper, you said that you've never

26 exposed classified information in an inappropriate

27 manner. I asked Director Comey these questions last

28 week, so for both of you, yes or no. As far as you

29 know, has any classified information relating to Mr.

1 Trump or his associates been declassified and shared
2 with the media?
3
4 **CLAPPER:** Not to my knowledge.
5
6 **GRASSLEY:** Ms. Yates?
7
8 **YATES**: Not to my knowledge either.
9
10 **GRASSLEY:** OK. Next question; have either of you
11 ever been an anonymous source in a news report
12 about matters relating to Mr. Trump, his associates or
13 Russia's attempt to meddle in the election?
14
15 **CLAPPER:** No.
16
17 **YATES**: Absolutely not.
18
19 **GRASSLEY:** OK. Third question; did either of you
20 ever authorize someone else at your respective
21 organizations to be an anonymous source in a news
22 report about Mr. Trump or his associates?
23
24 **CLAPPER:** No.
25
26 **YATES**: No.
27
28 **GRASSLEY:** OK. As far as either of you know, have
29 any government agencies referred any of the leaks

1 over the past several months to the Justice
2 Department for potential criminal investigation?
3
4 **CLAPPER:** I don't know. As you know, Senator, there
5 is a process
6 for that -- for doing that. I don't know if that -- that's
7 happened.
8
9 **GRASSLEY:** Ms. Yates?
10
11 **YATES**: I'm not at DOJ anymore, so I don't know
12 what's been referred.
13
14 **GRASSLEY:** So then I guess to kind of sum up,
15 neither one of you know whether the department
16 authorized a criminal investigation of the leaks?
17
18 **CLAPPER:** I do not, sir.
19
20 **YATES**: No, sir.
21
22 **GRASSLEY:** OK. Have any of you been questioned
23 by the FBI about any leaks?
24
25 **CLAPPER:** I have not been.
26
27 **YATES**: No.
28
29 **GRASSLEY:** OK. I want to discuss unmasking.

1   Mr. Clapper and Ms. Yates, did either of you ever
2   request the unmasking of Mr. Trump, his associates
3   or any member of Congress?
4
5   **CLAPPER:** Yes, in one case I did that I can specifically
6   recall, but I can't discuss it any further than that.
7
8   **GRASSLEY:** You can't, so if I ask you for details, you
9   said you can't discuss that, is that what you said?
10
11   **CLAPPER:** Not -- not here.
12
13   **GRASSLEY:** OK.
14   Ms. Yates, can you answer that question? Did you
15   ever request unmasking of Mr. Trump, his associates
16   or any member of Congress?
17
18   **YATES**: No.
19
20   **GRASSLEY:** Question two. Did either of you ever
21   review classified documents in which Mr. Trump, his
22   associates or members of Congress had been
23   unmasked?
24
25   **CLAPPER:** Yes.
26
27   **GRASSLEY:** You have? Can you give us details here
28   in this...
29
30   **CLAPPER:** No, I can't.

1
2   **GRASSLEY:** Ms. Yates, have you?
3
4   **YATES:** Yes, I have and no, I can't give you details.
5
6   **GRASSLEY:** OK. Did either of you ever share
7   information about unmasked (ph) Trump associates
8   or members of Congress with anyone else?
9
10   **CLAPPER:** Well, I'm thinking back over six and a half
11   years, I could have discussed it with either my deputy
12   or my general counsel.
13
14   **GRASSLEY:** Ms. Yates?
15
16   **YATES:** In the course of the Flynn matter, I had
17   discussions with other members of the intel
18   community. I'm not sure if that's responsive to your
19   question.
20
21   **GRASSLEY:** And in both cases, you can't give details
22   here.
23
24   **YATES:** No.
25
26   **CLAPPER:** No.
27
28   **GRASSLEY:** The FBI notified the Democratic
29   National Committee of the Russian's intrusion into
30   their systems in August of 2015, but the DNC turned

down the FBI's offer to get the Russians out and refused the FBI access to their servers. Instead, it evidently eventually hired a private firm in the spring of 2016. WikiLeaks began releasing the hacked DNC e-mails last July. It took roughly 27,000 of the 27,500 DNC e-mails it released were e-mails sent after the FBI notified the DNC of the breach.

Mr. Clapper, would you agree that one of the lessons of this episode is that people should cooperate with the FBI when notified of foreign hacks instead of stone walling?

CLAPPER: Yes, sir. I generally think that's a very good idea.

GRASSLEY: Mr. Clapper, you sent the Russians -- you said the Russians did not release any negative information on Republican candidates. I believe that that's not quite right. On June the 15th, 2016, Guccifer 2.0 released to Gawker and The Smoking Gun more than 200 pages of the DNC's opposition research on Mr. Trump's -- hundreds of pages of what I would call dirt. This happened just two days after The Wall Street Journal published a plan for Republican Convention delegates to revolt to prevent Mr. Trump from securing the nomination.

Why wasn't - why wasn't the Russian release of harmful information about Mr. Trump addressed in

1   the Russia report? And was this even evaluated
2   during the review?
3

4   **CLAPPER:** I would have to consult with the analysts
5   that were involved in the report to definitively
6   answer that. I don't know personally whether they
7   considered that or not.
8

9   **GRASSLEY:** Can you submit that as an answer in
10   writing?
11

12   **CLAPPER:** Well, I'm a private citizen now, sir. I don't
13   know what -- what the rules are on my...
14

15   **GRASSLEY:** Well, give me the name...
16

17   **CLAPPER:** ... obtaining classified -- potentially
18   classified information, so I will look in to it.
19

20   **GRASSLEY:** OK. Mr. Clapper, you testified that the
21   intelligence community conducted an exhaustive
22   review of Russian interference and the analysts
23   involved had complete, unfettered access to all
24   sensitive raw intelligence data. Do you have any
25   reason to believe that any agency withheld any
26   relevant information?
27

28   **CLAPPER:** I don't believe so, with one potential
29   caveat, which is that there is the possibility, again
30   acknowledging this role that the FBI plays in

straddling both intelligence and law enforcement, that for whatever reason they may have chosen to withhold investigatory sensitive information from the report. I don't know that to be a fact. I was not apprised of that, I'm just suggesting that as a possibility.

GRASSLEY: My time's up, Mr. Chairman. Thank you.

GRAHAM: Thank you.
Senator Feinstein.

FEINSTEIN: Thanks very much, Mr. Chairman.
Ms. Yates, I'm not going to ask you anything that deserves a confidential or secure answer, but after your second in-person meeting with Mr. McGahn, you said there were four topics he wanted to discuss. Would you list those four topics?

YATES: Sure. The first topic in the second meeting was essentially why does it matter to DOJ if one White House official lies to another. The second topic related to the applicability of criminal statutes and the likelihood that the Department of Justice would pursue a criminal case. The third topic was his concern that their taking action might interfere with an investigation of Mr. Flynn. And the fourth topic was his request to see the underlying evidence.

1   **FEINSTEIN:** Were all those topics satisfied with
2   respect to your impression after the second meeting?
3

4   **YATES:** Yes. The only thing that was really left open
5   there would (ph) -- was the logistics, for us to be able
6   to make arrangements for them to look at the
7   underlying evidence.
8

9   **FEINSTEIN:** And you did make those arrangements?
10

11   **YATES:** We did make those arrangements, but again,
12   I don't know whether that ever happened, whether
13   they ever looked at...
14

15   **FEINSTEIN:** OK.
16

17   **YATES:** ... that evidence or not.
18

19   **FEINSTEIN:** Fair enough.
20   Apparently, Lieutenant General Flynn remained
21   national security adviser for 18 days after you raised
22   the Justice Department's concern. In your view,
23   during those 18 days, did the risk that Flynn had been
24   or could be compromised diminish at all?
25

26   **YATES:** You know, I don't know that I'm in a position
27   to really have an answer for that. I know that we were
28   really concerned about the compromise here, and that
29   was the reason why we were encouraging them to act.

1 I don't know what steps they may have taken, if any,
2 during that 18 days to minimize any risk.
3
4 **FEINSTEIN:** Well, did you discuss this with other
5 DOJ career professionals?
6
7 **YATES:** Certainly, leading up to our notification on
8 the 26th. It was a topic of a whole lot of discussion, in
9 DOJ and with other members of the intel community,
10 and we discussed it at great length. But after the 30th,
11 again, I wasn't at DOJ anymore, so I didn't have any
12 further discussions after that point about what was
13 being done with respect to that.
14
15 **FEINSTEIN:** Did you consult with other career
16 prosecutors?
17
18 **YATES:** Absolutely. We had, really, the experts
19 within the national security division. As we were
20 navigating this situation, they were working with the
21 FBI on the investigation, and we were trying to make
22 a determination about how best to make this
23 notification so that we could get the information to
24 the White House that they needed to be able to act.
25
26 **FEINSTEIN:** So what's the point that you were trying
27 to make -- yes or no will be fine -- that General Flynn
28 had seriously compromised the security of the United
29 States, and possibly the government, by what he had
30 done, whatever that was?

1

2   **YATES**: Well, our point was -- is that logic would tell

3   you that you don't want the national security adviser

4   to be in a position where the Russians have leverage

5   over him. Now, in terms of

6   what impact that may have or could have had, I can't

7   speak to that, but we knew that was not a good

8   situation, which is why we wanted to let the White

9   House know about it.

10

11   **FEINSTEIN:** The Guardian has reported that Britain's

12   intelligence service first became aware in late 2015 of

13   suspicious interactions between Trump advisers and

14   Russian intelligence agents. This information was

15   passed on to U.S. intelligence agencies.

16   Over the spring of 2016, multiple European allies

17   passed on additional information to the United States

18   about contacts between the Trump campaign and

19   Russians. Is this accurate?

20

21   **YATES**: I -- I can't answer that.

22

23   **FEINSTEIN:** General Clapper, is that accurate?

24

25   **CLAPPER:** Yes, it is and it's also quite sensitive.

26

27   **FEINSTEIN:** OK. Let me ask you this.

28

29   **CLAPPER:** The specifics are -- are --- are quite

30   sensitive.

1

2 **FEINSTEIN:** When did components of the

3 intelligence community open investigations into the

4 interactions between trump advisers and Russians?

5 What was the question again, ma'am, I'm sorry?

6

7 **FEINSTEIN:** When did components of the

8 intelligence community open investigations into the

9 interactions between Trump advisers and Russians?

10

11 **CLAPPER:** What was the question, again, Ma'am? I'm

12 sorry.

13

14 **FEINSTEIN:** When did components of the

15 intelligence community open investigations into the

16 interactions between Trump advisers and Russians?

17

18 **CLAPPER:** Well, I can -- I refer to Director Comey's

19 statement before the House Intelligence Committee

20 on the 20th of March -- is when he advised that they'd

21 open an investigation in July of '16.

22

23 **FEINSTEIN:** And what was the reaction when you

24 advised that the investigation be opened as early as

25 July 15th?

26

27 **CLAPPER:** I'm sorry?

28

29 **FEINSTEIN:** I -- I thought you said that you advised

30 on July...

1

2　**CLAPPER:** No, Director Comey did, before the House
3　Intelligence Committee...

4

5　**FEINSTEIN:** The director (ph) -- I see.

6

7　**CLAPPER:** ... announced that the FBI had initiated
8　investigation in July of 2016.

9

10　**FEINSTEIN:** Well, what did the intelligence agencies
11　do with the findings that I just spoke about that The
12　Guardian wrote about?

13

14　**CLAPPER:** Well, I'm not sure about the accuracy of
15　that article, so clearly over actually going back to
16　2015, there was evidence of Soviet, excuse me,
17　Freudian slip, Russian activity. Mainly, in an
18　information gathering or recon ordering mode, where
19　they were investigating voter registration rolls and
20　the like.

21

22　And that activity started early, and so, we were
23　monitoring this as it progressed, and certainly as it
24　picked up, accelerated in spring, summer and fall of
25　2016.

26

27　**FEINSTEIN:** OK.
28　So let me go back to you, Miss Yates, I take it you
29　were very concerned. What was your prime worry
30　during all of this? Now, you were worried that

1 General Flynn would be compromised? What did you
2 think would happen, if he were, and how do you
3 believe he would have been compromised?
4
5 **YATES**: Well, we had two concerns, compromise was
6 certainly the number one concern and the Russians
7 can use compromised material, information, in a
8 variety of ways, sometimes overtly and sometimes
9 subtly. And again, our concern was, is that you have a
10 very sensitive position, like the National Security
11 advisor and you don't want that person to be in a
12 position, where again, the Russians have leverage
13 over him.
14
15 But, I will also say, another motivating factor is that
16 we felt like the Vice President was entitled to know
17 that the information he had been given, and that he
18 was relaying to the American public, wasn't true.
19
20 **FEINSTEIN:** So, what's you're saying is that General
21 Flynn lied to the Vice President?
22
23 **YATES**: That's certainly how it appeared, yes,
24 because the Vice President went out and made
25 statements about General Flynn's conduct, that he
26 said were based on what General Flynn had told him,
27 and we knew that that just flat wasn't true.
28
29 **FEINSTEIN:** Well, as the days went on, what was
30 your view of the situation? Because there were, I

1   guess two weeks before, or was it 18 days before
2   Director Flynn was dismissed?
3
4   **YATES**: Well, again, I was no longer with DOJ after
5   the 30th, and so I wasn't having interaction or any
6   involvement in this issue after that day.
7
8   **FEINSTEIN:** Thank you, Mr. Chairman.
9
10 **GRAHAM:** Senator Cornyn.
11
12 **SEN. JOHN CORNYN, R-TEXAS:** Thank you,
13 Chairman Graham.
14
15 And Senator Whitehouse, for today's hearing.
16 This is important, the American people have every
17 right to know as much as possible about Russian
18 interference in our elections. But, as I think, as the
19 Director has told us before many times, this is not
20 anything new.
21
22 Although, perhaps, the level and intensity, and the
23 sophistication, of both Russian overt and covert
24 operations is really unprecedented, and I thank the
25 intelligence community for their assessment.
26
27 I do regret that, while these two witnesses are
28 certainly welcomed and we're glad to have them here,
29 that former National Security Advisor Susan Rice, has
30 refused to testify in front of the Committee. It seems

1 to me, there are a lot of questions that she needs to
2 answer.
3
4 I would point out, though, Mr. Chairman, that both
5 Senator Feinstein and I, are fortunate enough to be on
6 the Senate Intelligence Committee, which is also
7 conducting a bipartisan investigation under the
8 leadership of Chairman Burr and Vice Chairman
9 Warner.
10
11 One of the benefits of that additional investigation, is
12 that we have been given access to the raw intelligence
13 collected by the intelligence community, which I
14 think, completes what understandably is an
15 incomplete picture. When you can only talk in a
16 public setting about part of the evidence, but it is
17 important for the American people to understand
18 what's happening.
19
20 I think this subcommittee hearing is playing an
21 important role in that.
22
23 I want to ask Director Clapper, because, I think,
24 unfortunately some of the discussion about
25 unmasking is casting suspicion on the intelligence
26 community in a way that I think is, frankly,
27 concerning. Particularly when we're looking at
28 reauthorizing Section 702 of the Patriot Act by the end
29 of next year,

1 because as many have said, I can't recall your specific
2 words, but I know Director Comey has called that the
3 crown jewels of the intelligence community, and I'm
4 very concerned that some of the information that's
5 been discussed about unmasking, for example, might
6 cause some people to worry about their legitimate
7 privacy concerns.
8
9 **CORNYN:** So when it comes to incidental collection
10 on an American person, and that is unmasked at the
11 request of some appropriate authority, can you
12 describe, briefly, the paper trail and the series -- and
13 the approval process that is required in order to allow
14 that to happen? That's not a trivial matter, is it?
15
16 **CLAPPER:** The -- and the -- the process is that, first of
17 all, the judgment as to whether or not to unmask or
18 reveal the identity is rendered by the original
19 collection agency so normally that's going to be, in the
20 case of 702 -- going to be NSA.
21
22 And I know, for my part, because, as I indicated in
23 my statement, over my six and a half years of DNI, I
24 occasionally ask for identities to be unmasked to
25 understand the context.
26
27 What I was concerned about, and those of us in the
28 intelligence community are concerned about, is the
29 behavior of the -- the validated foreign intelligence

1	target. Is that target trying to co-opt, recruit, bribe,
2	penetrate or what?
3	
4	And it's very difficult to understand that context by
5	the labels "U.S. person one," "U.S. person two." And
6	as well, I should point out, doing that on an anecdotal
7	basis, one SIGINT report at a time, in which you need
8	to look at is there a -- is there a pattern here, and so I
9	tried on my part to be very, very judicious about that.
10	
11	It's a very sensitive thing. But I did feel an obligation,
12	as DNI, that I should attempt to understand the
13	context and who this person was, because that had a
14	huge bearing on how important or critical it was, and
15	what threat might be posed by virtue of the -- again,
16	the behavior of the validated foreign intelligence
17	target.
18	
19	So our focus was on the target, not -- not as much as
20	the U.S. person -- only to understand the context.
21	
22	**CORNYN:** Well, the fact that some appropriate
23	authority might request and receive the unmasking of
24	the name of the U.S. person does not then authorize
25	the release of that information -- that classified
26	information -- into the public domain? that remains a
27	crime, does it not?
28	
29	**CLAPPER:** Yes. Again, that's why I attempted to
30	make -- to clarify, in my statement...

1
2   **(CROSSTALK)**
3
4 <u>**CORNYN (?):**</u> Push the button.
5
6 <u>**CLAPPER:**</u> That's why, in my statement, I attempted
7 to make that distinction between unmasking, an
8 authorized, legitimate process with approval by the
9 appropriate authorities, and leaking, which is an
10 unauthorized process under any circumstance.
11
12 <u>**CORNYN:**</u> Mr. Chairman, I think it's really important
13 that, in order to determine who actually requested the
14 unmasking, and in order to establish whether
15 appropriate procedures were undertaken under both
16 legislative oversight and judicial oversight, that we
17 determine what that paper trail is and follow it...
18
19 <u>**CLAPPER:**</u> Senator Cornyn, if I may, I just -- and I
20 have to be very careful here about how I phrase this,
21 but I would just repeat to you the definition of what
22 702 is used for...
23
24 <u>**CORNYN:**</u> Foreign intelligence (ph).
25
26 <u>**CLAPPER:**</u> ... which is collection against a non-U.S.
27 person overseas.
28

1 **CORNYN:** I don't think you can say that enough,
2 Director Clapper. It's important, because people need
3 to understand that...

5 **CLAPPER:** Happy to say it again.

7 **CORNYN:** ... we are both getting necessary foreign
8 intelligence...

10 **(CROSSTALK)**

12 **CORNYN:** ... to keep the American people safe, but
13 also respecting the privacy rights and the
14 constitutional rights of American citizens.

16 **CLAPPER:** Absolutely.

18 **CORNYN:** Ms. Yates, this is the first time that you've
19 appeared before Congress since you left the
20 Department of Justice, and I just wanted to ask you a
21 question about the -- your decision to refuse to defend
22 the president's executive order.

24 In the letter that you sent to Congress, you point out
25 that the executive order itself was drafted in
26 consultation with the Office of Legal Counsel, and
27 you point out that the Office of Legal Counsel
28 reviewed it to determine whether, in its view, the
29 proposed executive order was lawful on its face and
30 properly drafted.

1

2 Is it true that the Office of Legal Counsel did conclude

3 it was lawful on its face and properly drafted?

4

5 **YATES**: Yes, they did. The office of...

6

7 **CORNYN:** And you overruled them?

8

9 **YATES**: ... I did. The office of legal...

10

11 **CORNYN:** Did you (ph) -- what -- what is your

12 authority to -- to overrule the Office of Legal Counsel

13 when it comes to a legal determination?

14

15 **YATES**: The Office of Legal Counsel has a narrow

16 function, and that is to look at the face of an executive

17 order and to determine purely on its face whether

18 there is some set of circumstances under which at

19 least some part of the executive order may be lawful.

20 And importantly, they do not look beyond the face of

21 the executive order, for example, statement that are

22 made contemporaneously or prior to the execution of

23 the E.O. that may bear on its intent and purpose.

24

25 That office does not look at those factors, and in

26 determining the constitutionality of this executive

27 order, that was an important analysis to engage in

28 and one that I did.

29

1   **CORNYN:** Well, Ms. Yates, I thought the Department

2   of Justice had a long standing tradition of defending a

3   presidential action in court if there are reasonable

4   arguments in its favor, regardless whether those

5   arguments might prove to be ultimately persuasive,

6   which of course is up to the courts to decide and not

7   you, correct?

8

9   **YATES:** It is correct that often times, but not always,

10   the civil division of the Department of Justice will

11   defend an action of the president or an action of

12   Congress if there is a reasonable argument to be

13   made. But in this instance, all - all arguments have to

14   be based on truth because we're the Department of

15   Justice. We're not just a law firm, we're the

16   Department of Justice and the...

17

18   **(CROSSTALK)**

19

20   **CORNYN:** You distinguish the truth from lawful?

21

22   **YATES:** Yes, because in this instance, in looking at

23   what the intent was of the executive order, which was

24   derived in part from an analysis of facts outside the

25   face of the order, that is part of what led to our

26   conclusion that it was not lawful, yes.

27

28   **CORNYN:** Well, Ms. Yates, you had a distinguished

29   career for 27 years at the Department of Justice and I

30   voted for your confirmation because I believed that

1 you had a distinguished career. But I have to tell you
2 that I find it enormously disappointing that you
3 somehow vetoed the decision of the Office of Legal
4 Counsel with regard to the lawfulness of the
5 president's order and decided instead that you would
6 counter man (ph) the executive order of the president
7 of the United States because you happen to disagree
8 with it as a policy matter.
9
10 **YATES**: Well, it was...
11
12 **CORNYN:** I just have to say that.
13
14 **YATES**: I appreciate that, Senator, and let me make
15 one thing clear. It is not purely as a policy matter. In
16 fact, I'll remember my confirmation hearing. In an
17 exchange that I had with you and others of your
18 colleagues where you specifically asked me in that
19 hearing that if the president asked me to do
20 something that was unlawful or unconstitutional and
21 one of your colleagues said or even just that would
22 reflect poorly on the Department of Justice, would I
23 say no? And I looked at this, I made a determination
24 that I believed that it was unlawful. I also thought
25 that it was inconsistent with principles of the
26 Department of Justice and I said no. And that's what I
27 promised you I would do and that's what I did.
28
29 **CORNYN:** I don't know how you can say that it was
30 lawful and say that it was within your prerogative to

1 refuse to defend it in a court of law and leave it to the
2 court to decide.
3
4 **YATES**: Senator, I did not say it was lawful. I said it
5 was unlawful.
6
7 **GRAHAM:** Senator Durbin is next, but I have one
8 quick, if you don't mind Senator Durbin, about how
9 702 works. You said something, General Clapper, I
10 don't quite understand. Is it unlawful to surveil with
11 a FISA warrant a foreign agent in the United States?
12
13 **CLAPPER:** No, it's not. But that's another provision. I
14 was - I was saying...
15
16 **GRAHAM:** OK.
17
18 **CLAPPER:** I was saying what 702 does.
19
20 **GRAHAM:** I just want to make sure there is a
21 procedure to do that.
22
23 **CLAPPER:** There is.
24
25 **GRAHAM:** OK.
26 Senator Durbin?
27 (UNKNOWN): Just to your point, you said the word
28 overseas. Ambassador Kislyak was not overseas on
29 December 29th, was he?
30

1   **CLAPPER:** That's correct.

2

3   **(UNKNOWN):** Thank you.

4

5   **SEN. RICHARD J. DURBIN, D-ILL.:** Thank you, Mr.
6   Chairman.
7   Let me say at the outset in response to Senator
8   Cornyn, in your conclusion about the unlawful nature
9   of the Muslim travel ban was, of course, a position
10   which was supported by three different federal courts
11   that stopped the enforcement of that ban and
12   ultimately led to the president withdrawing that
13   particular travel ban. Is that not true?

14

15   **YATES:** That's correct.

16

17   **DURBIN:** Thank you.
18   I want to mention at the outset here that this is a
19   critically important hearing and I want to thank
20   Senator Graham and Senator Whitehouse for the
21   bipartisan nature and the cooperation in this hearing.
22   I think the testimony we've received from these
23   witnesses and the presence of so many other of my
24   colleagues is an indication of how we view the
25   severity and gravity of the issue before us.

26

27   I'm troubled that this great committee with its great
28   chairman and all its members does not have
29   professional staff assigned to this investigation. It's
30   the ordinary staff of the subcommittee who are

1 working it. I think that what we have seen with this
2 situation calls for the appointment of an independent
3 commission,   presidential   commission   or
4 congressional   commission,   one   that   is   clearly
5 independent, transparent and can get to the bottom of
6 the Russian involvement in our last election process
7 and the threat that faces -- we face in the future
8 because of it.
9
10 Short of that, we'll continue to do our best on a
11 committee level with meager resources in both the
12 Intelligence Committee and here. And this is, I think,
13 an issue that begs for so much more. I might also say
14 that I'm starting to hear from the Republican side of
15 the table some real concerns about Section 702, which
16 Senator Lee, Republican member of the committee
17 and myself, have been calling for reform on for
18 several years. Unfortunately, we didn't have the
19 support from the other side of the table when we did.
20 I hope that we can get it now when we talk about real
21 reform to (ph) the 702 and protecting the rights of
22 individuals in America.
23
24 Ms. Yates, let me ask you about this meeting on
25 January the 26th with White House Counsel Don
26 McGahn. You shared the Justice Department's
27 concern about his communications with Russia, his
28 apparent dishonesty about those communications and
29 his vulnerability to blackmail. Is that correct?
30

1   **YATES**: That's right.

2

3   **DURBIN:** Was there anything else about the
4   relationship of General Flynn and the Russians other
5   than his representations that he had no conversation
6   that you warned Don McGahn about?

7

8   **YATES**: No.

9

10 **DURBIN:** So it didn't go back to his trip to Moscow,
11 money received and so forth?

12

13 **YATES**: No, it did not.

14

15 **DURBIN:** It was strictly on that question?

16

17 **YATES**: Yes.

18

19 **DURBIN:** And then you had a second meeting the
20 next day.

21

22 **YATES**: That's right.

23

24 **DURBIN:** Is that correct, on January 27th?

25

26 **YATES**: At his request, yes.

27

28 **DURBIN:** At Mr. McGahn's request. And at that
29 second meeting, did Mr. McGahn say anything about

1   whether he had taken the information you'd given

2   him the previous day to the president?

3

4   **YATES**: No, he didn't tell us.

5

6   **DURBIN:** Are you aware of the fact that Mr. Spicer,

7   the White House press secretary, on February 14th

8   said, and I quote, "Immediately after the Department

9   of Justice notified the White House counsel of the

10   situation, the White House counsel briefed the

11   president and a small group of senior advisors?"

12

13   **YATES**: I've seen media reports to that effect, but

14   that's all I know is from the media.

15

16   **DURBIN:** So there was no statement by Mr. McGahn

17   that he had either spoken to the president about your

18   concerns with his national security advisor or with

19   any other members of the White House?

20

21   **YATES**: No, he didn't advise us in the second meeting

22   anyone he may have discussed this with the prior

23   evening.

24

25   **DURBIN:** I guess I want to also go to the question

26   which keeps gnawing at me here that Mr. McGahn

27   asked of you. Is there anything wrong with one White

28   House official lying to another White House official?

29

YATES: Well, to be fair to Mr. McGahn here, I wouldn't say that he said is there anything wrong. His question was more essentially what's it to the Justice Department if one White House official is lying to another? In other words, why is this something that DOJ would be concerned about? And that's why went back through the list of issues and reasons why this was troubling to us.

DURBIN: Did you think there was a legal reason to be concerned if one White House official lied to another White House official?

YATES: We didn't go into that. And to the extent you may be talking about like 1001 violation, that was not something that we were alluding to or discussing with Mr. McGahn. I think his point when he made that point to me was that he wasn't sure why the Department of Justice would care about one lying to another, not to be discussing whether that was in fact a crime.

DURBIN: And the reason you told him was what?

YATES: Was that, again, it was a whole lot more than one White House official lying to another. First of all, it was the vice president of the United States and the vice president had then gone out and provided that information to the American people who had then

1 been misled and the Russians knew all of this, making
2 Mike Flynn compromised now.

4 **DURBIN:** You said earlier, I believe, that Mr.
5 McGahn asked you if you thought they should fire
6 General Flynn at that point.

8 **YATES**: Right.

10 **DURBIN:** And what was your response?

12 **YATES**: Told him that it was not our call as to
13 whether General Flynn was fired, that we were giving
14 them this information so that they could take action,
15 the action that they believed was appropriate.

17 **DURBIN:** On February 14th, after General Flynn
18 resigned, Sean Spicer said, and I quote, "There was
19 nothing in what General Flynn did in terms of
20 conducting himself that was an issue." Do you have
21 any idea what he meant by those words?

23 **YATES**: No. I'm not -- all I can say is he didn't reach
24 that conclusion from his conversation with us. I can't
25 speak to how he arrived at that.

27 **DURBIN:** Let me ask you, there was a period of time,
28 18 days, that we've referred to (inaudible) and during
29 that period of 18 days, a number of things occurred;
30 General Glynn continued to serve as the national

1　security advisor for 18 days after you had briefed the
2　White House about the counterintelligence risk that
3　he posed. And during those 18 days, General Flynn
4　continued to hire key senior staff on the National
5　Security Council, announced new sanctions on Iran's
6　ballistic missile program, met with Japanese Prime
7　Minister Shinzo Abe along with President Trump at
8　Mar-a-Lago and participated in discussions about
9　responding to a North Korean missile launch and
10　spoke repeatedly to the press about his
11　communications with Russian Ambassador Kisliak.
12

13　**DURBIN:** Ms. Yates, in -- in your view, were there
14　national security concerns in these decisions being
15　made after the information you shared with the White
16　House?
17

18　**YATES**: I was no long with DOJ after January 30th, so
19　I wasn't aware of any actions that the General Flynn
20　was taking. So I -- I couldn't really opine on that.
21

22　**DURBIN:** General Clapper? Would you comment? If
23　you had the warning from the White House -- pardon
24　me, from the Department of Justice to the White
25　House about General Flynn possibly being
26　compromised here, and then these important national
27　security decisions had followed, would you have
28　concern about that?
29

1   **CLAPPER:** Well, I would. Hypothetically, yes. I
2   mean, again, I was gone from the government as well
3   when all this happened.
4
5   **DURBIN:** But -- but you've had quite a career in
6   intelligence and national security. And here, you have
7   a man that's been told -- the White House has been
8   told his -- he could be compromised and blackmailed
9   by the Russians -- continuing to make the highest
10   level decisions of our government.
11
12   **CLAPPER:** Well, that's -- that's -- it is certainly a
13   potential vulnerability, there's no question about it.
14
15   **DURBIN:** I would say so. Thank you very much.
16   Thanks, Mr. Chairman.
17
18   **GRAHAM:** (OFF-MIKE)
19
20   **SEN. TED CRUZ, R-TEXAS:** Thank you, Mr.
21   Chairman. Thank you to the witnesses for being here
22   today.
23
24   Mr. Clapper, you -- you testified as to the harms that
25   come from leaks -- the harms that come to our
26   national security -- and you also testified about the
27   importance of protecting classified information and
28   keeping it classified.
29

During your many years in intelligence, and at the DNI, have you ever knowingly forwarded classified information to a non-government employee on a non-government computer who did not have authorization to receive that information?

CLAPPER: Not to my -- not to my recollection, no, sir.

CRUZ: And, Director Clapper, what would you do, at the DNI, if you discovered that an employee of yours had forwarded hundreds or even thousands of e-mails to a non-government individual, their spouse, on a non-government computer?

CLAPPER: Well, you know, I'm not a investigatory or prosecutorial element. But if I were aware of it, I would certainly make known to the appropriate officials that that was going on.

CRUZ: Would that strike you as anything ordinary?

CLAPPER: Hopefully not.

CRUZ: What -- what concerns would that raise for you?

CLAPPER: Well, it raises all kinds of potential security concerns. Again, depending on -- on the -- the content of the e-mail, what the intent was, there's a whole bunch of variables here that would have to be

1 considered. But, you know, potentially, and again,
2 this is a hypothetical scenario, it could be quite
3 concerning.
4
5 **CRUZ:** What would you expect to happen if you
6 made a referral of an individual who had forwarded
7 hundreds or even thousands of classified
8 information...
9
10 **CLAPPER:** Well...
11
12 **CRUZ:** ... to a non-government employee...
13
14 **CLAPPER:** ... whether (ph)...
15
16 **CRUZ:** ... on a non-government computer?
17
18 **CLAPPER:** ... whatever the transgression -- potential
19 transgression was, if there were sufficient evidence of
20 a compromise, we would file a crimes report. That's
21 standard procedure that we use when there's the
22 potential for investigating and prosecuting someone.
23
24 **CRUZ:** Last week, I asked similar questions to FBI
25 Director Comey, and -- and he said an individual who
26 did that would be subject to, quote, "significant
27 administrative discipline," but that he was highly
28 confident they wouldn't be prosecuted. Do you share
29 that assessment?
30

1   **CLAPPER:** Well, I don't -- I -- I don't know. I think the
2   -- the track record is that the prior administration, I
3   think, prosecuted more people for leaking than
4   anyone in any -- in any other administration in the
5   past.
6
7   So it's difficult to do that. And there are many cases
8   we could not prosecute or even seek a crimes report
9   because the potential audience of people that could
10   have been the perpetrator of -- of -- of these
11   insecurities could not be identified.
12
13   **CRUZ:** It is true that other individuals who were not
14   the direct employee of the Democratic nominee for
15   president were prosecuted for that conduct. Let me --
16   let me shift to a different topic.
17
18   Director Clapper, you -- you also testified that you're
19   not aware of any intercepted communications of any
20   presidential candidates or campaigns, other than the
21   Trump campaign that's been discussed here. Is -- is
22   that correct?
23
24   **CLAPPER:** Yes. But that's to my knowledge. But, you
25   know, prior administrations, prior campaigns -- they
26   wouldn't have been visible to me. So I -- I can't -- I
27   can't say...
28
29   **CRUZ:** But -- but in 2016, you're not aware any other
30   campaigns or candidates?

1

2 **CLAPPER:** ... no.

3

4 **CRUZ:** And, Ms. Yates, same question to you.

5

6 **YATES**: I'm not aware of any interceptions of the
7 Trump campaign.

8

9 **CRUZ:** And are you aware of any intercepted
10 communications of any other candidates or
11 campaigns?

12

13 **YATES**: No.

14

15 **CRUZ:** Okay. Because earlier, when Chairman
16 Graham had asked you that, I -- I thought you'd
17 declined to answer. So perhaps I misunderstood that.

18

19 **YATES**: And I may have misunderstood the question.
20 I thought the question I declined to answer was a
21 different one than that. So I'm -- I'm glad I got a
22 chance to clear it up.

23

24 **CRUZ:** OK. So you have no information of any
25 interceptions of the Bernie Sanders campaign, Hillary
26 Clinton campaign...

27

28 **YATES**: No.

29

30 **CRUZ:** ... or any other candidate...

1

2   **YATES**: No.

3

4   **CRUZ:** ... in 2016, or campaigns? **YATES**: No.

5

6   **CRUZ:** OK. Let' revisit the topic, Ms. Yates, that --
7   that you and Senator Cornyn were talking about.

8

9   **YATES**: OK.

10

11   **CRUZ:** It is correct that the constitution vests the
12   executive authority in the president?

13

14   **YATES**: Yes.

15

16   **CRUZ:** And if an attorney general disagrees with a
17   policy decision of the president -- a policy decision
18   that is lawful -- does the attorney general have the
19   authority to direct the Department of Justice to defy
20   the president's order?

21

22   **YATES**: I don't know whether the attorney general
23   has the authority to do that or not. But I don't think it
24   would be a good idea. And that's not what I did in
25   this case.

26

27   **CRUZ:** Well, are you familiar with 8 USC Section
28   1182?

29

30   **YATES**: Not off the top of my head, no.

1

2 **CRUZ:** Well, it -- it -- it is the binding statutory

3 authority for the executive order that you refused to

4 implement, and that led to your termination. So it -- it

5 certainly is a relevant and not a terribly obscure

6 statute.

7

8 By the express text of the statute, it says, quote,

9 "whenever the president finds that entry of any alien

10 or of any class of aliens into the United States would

11 be detrimental to the interest of the United States, he

12 may by proclamation, and for such period as he shall

13 deem necessary, suspend the entry of all aliens or any

14 class of aliens as immigrants or non-immigrants, or

15 impose on the entry of aliens any restrictions he may

16 deem appropriate."

17

18 Would you agree that is broad statutory

19 authorization?

20

21 **YATES**: I would, and I am familiar with that. And I'm

22 also familiar with an additional provision of the INA

23 that says no person shall receive preference or be

24 discriminated against an issuance of a visa because of

25 race, nationality or place of birth, that I believe was

26 promulgated after the statute that you just quoted.

27

28 And that's been part of the discussion with the courts,

29 with respect to the INA, is whether this more specific

30 statute trumps the first one that you just described.

1
2   **(CROSSTALK)**
3
4   <u>**YATES**</u>: But my concern was not an INA concern
5   here. It, rather, was a constitutional concern, whether
6   or not this -- the executive order here violated the
7   Constitution, specifically with the establishment
8   clause and equal protection and due process.
9
10   <u>**CRUZ:**</u> There is no doubt the arguments you laid out
11   are arguments that we could expect litigants to bring,
12   partisan litigants who disagree with the policy
13   decision of the president.
14
15   I would note, on January 27th, 2017, the Department
16   of Justice issued an official legal decision, a
17   determination by the Office of Legal Counsel, that the
18   executive order -- and I'll quote from the opinion --
19   "the proposed order is approved with respect to form
20   and legality."
21
22   That's a determination from OLC on January 27th that
23   it was legal. Three days later, you determined, using
24   your own words, that although OLC had -- had
25   opined on legality, it had not addressed whether it
26   was, quote, "wise or just."
27
28   <u>**YATES**</u>: And I also, in that same directive, Senator,
29   said that I was not convinced it was lawful. I also
30   made the point that the office of -- OLC looks purely

1 at the face of the document and, again, makes a
2 determination as to whether there is some set of
3 circumstances under which some portion of that E.O.
4 would be enforceable, would be lawful.
5
6 They, importantly, do not look outside the face of the
7 document. And in this particular instance,
8 particularly where we were talking about a
9 fundamental issue of religious freedom -- not the
10 interpretation of some arcane statute, but religious
11 freedom -- it was appropriate for us to look at the
12 intent behind the president's actions, and the intent is
13 laid in and out his statements.
14
15 **CRUZ:** A final, very -- very brief question. In the over
16 200 years of the Department of Justice history, are you
17 aware of any instance in which the Department of
18 Justice has formally approved the legality of a policy,
19 and three days later, the attorney general has directed
20 the department not to follow that policy, and to defy
21 that policy?
22
23 **YATES**: I'm not. But I'm also not aware of a situation
24 where the Office of Legal Counsel was advised not to
25 tell the attorney general about it until after it was
26 over.

www.ingramcontent.com/pod-product-compliance
Lightning Source LLC
Chambersburg PA
CBHW050423290526
45786CB00003B/1382